Belongs to
Jessica.H.S

S

My head-to-toe body book

My head-to-toe body book

Thames & Hudson

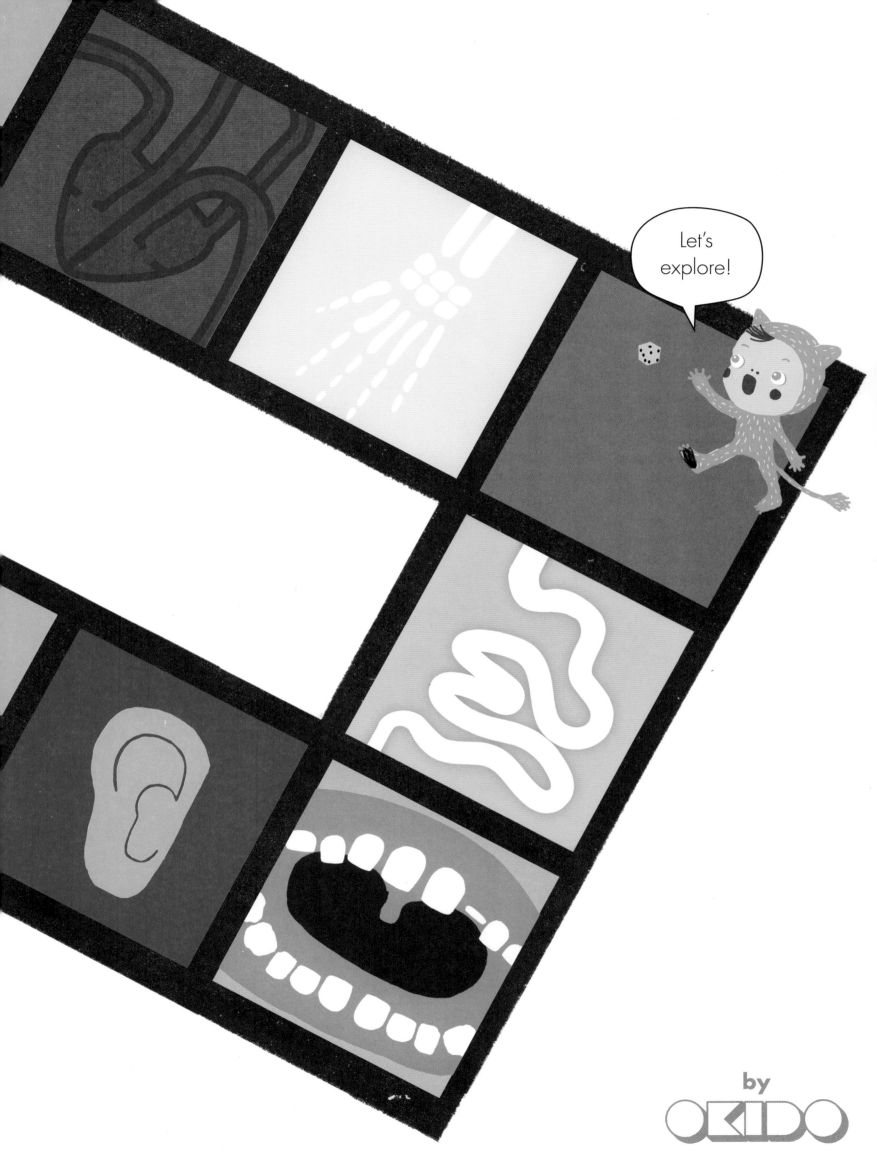

Questions from head to toe ...

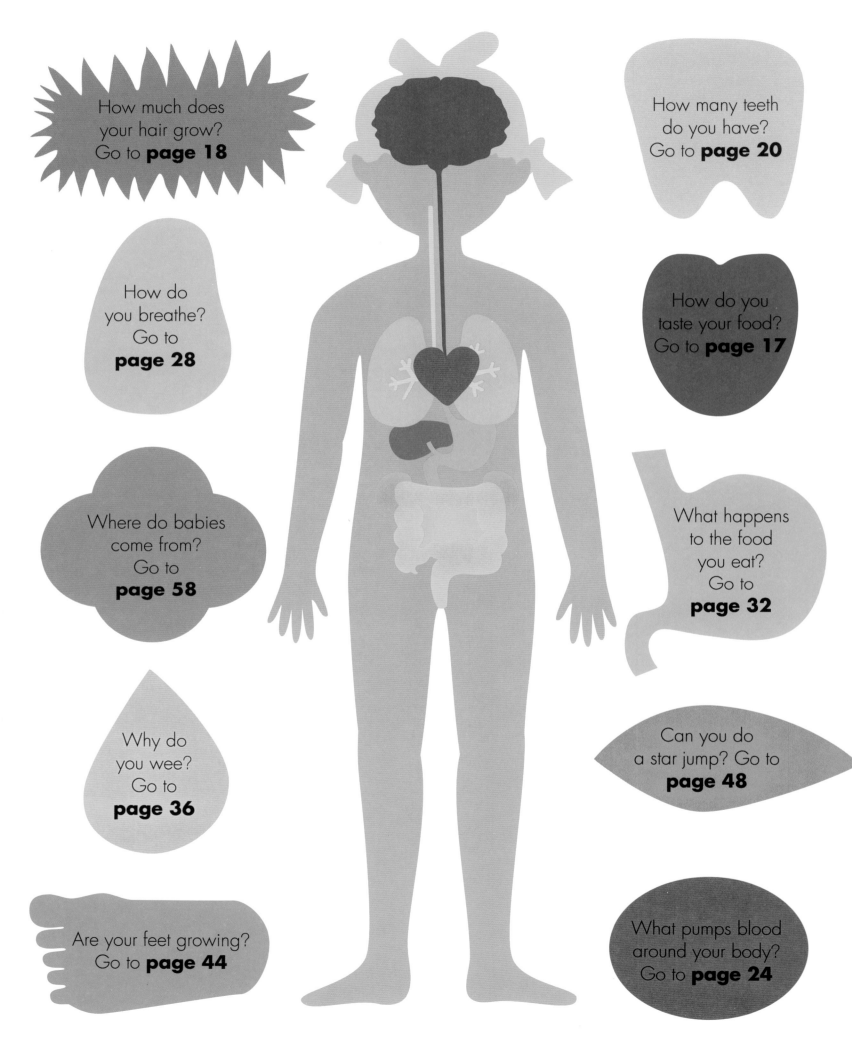

How much does your hair grow? Go to **page 18**

How many teeth do you have? Go to **page 20**

How do you breathe? Go to **page 28**

How do you taste your food? Go to **page 17**

Where do babies come from? Go to **page 58**

What happens to the food you eat? Go to **page 32**

Why do you wee? Go to **page 36**

Can you do a star jump? Go to **page 48**

Are your feet growing? Go to **page 44**

What pumps blood around your body? Go to **page 24**

Where to find out!

How to use this book

Are you ready to go on a journey through your body from top to toe, inside and out?

Say hello to Koko

Hi, I'm Koko. I'm your guide. I love finding out new things. Do you?

How tall are you? Measure this book against yourself. How many books high are you?

Hi, I'm Koko's friend Alex. I'm listening to my heartbeat. Put your hand to your chest to feel yours.

25 cm

20 cm

15 cm

10 cm

5 cm

When you see ...

... ask a grown-up to help you.

... get ready to do things.

Where next?
Your brain controls your muscles.
Go to **My muscles, page 46**

... go to another page to find out more.

Meet the explorers

The three explorers travel inside your body and show you how it works. They love adventures!

Look! It's this way. Everyone ready? Follow me!

Well, let me just check the map and find the way.

Come on guys, let's go! We've got lots of exploring to do.

OK! Let's go ...

My brain

Count from one to ten. Now move your legs and dance!

What makes you do these things? It's your brain – the part of your body that is in charge! This picture shows inside your brain.

Tap your head. That's your skull keeping your brain safe.

move

Hey! I've found the part of the brain you use to think.

think

I remember where I put my favourite toy. Where's yours?

remember

Different parts of your brain control different things, such as thinking. What else does your brain control?

Look! Messages are going up and down to the rest of the body.

feel

Look at all the
pictures in here!

see

Can you hear
the cymbals
crashing together?

hear

balance

Koko! Send
a message
to make this
leg move.
Thanks!

How does your brain tell your body what to do?

It sends messages to different parts of your body along paths called nerves. Then these parts send messages back to the brain.

●·········▶ send
●·········▶ receive

Let's pinch
this finger.
Can you
feel it Koko?

Where next?

Your brain controls your muscles.
Try it … stretch your legs.

Go to **My muscles, page 46**

9

Remote-control brain game

Play this game and find out how your brain controls your body.

You will need

cardboard, coloured pens, dressing-up clothes, a friend

1 Make a cardboard remote control. Write on simple orders. Dress up or stay in your everyday clothes.

2 Decide who is the brain and who is the body. Shout out orders – turn, jump up, grab a chair!

I am the body.
I do what
you say!

I am the brain.
I control you!
Lift up your arm.

up

down

grab

turn

Memory game

Use your brainpower! How good is your memory?

Look at the objects on the tray for one minute.
Try to remember them all.

Now turn the page ...

What is missing from the tray? Did you get it right?

Make your own game

Play with friends

You will need
paper plate
ten small objects

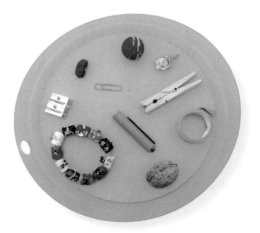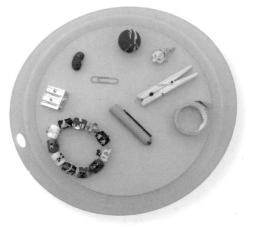

1 Ask a friend to look at the plate for one minute.

2 Without your friend seeing, take away one object. Can your friend remember which one is missing?

My senses

How can you tell what's safe and what's dangerous?

You use your senses. They tell you all about your world. You have five senses. They are taste, touch, smell, sight and hearing.

Alex can see the bird and hear it singing.

Match it

Can you tell which senses Alex is using? Match the words to the pictures. Which sense is he not using?

TOUCH
skin

SEE
eye

SMELL
nose

TASTE
tongue

HEAR
ear

My senses

Koko and her friend Alex are having a lovely picnic.

What animals can they **see** at the pond?

What prickly things should they not **touch**?

What sweet things can they **taste** for lunch?

What can they **hear** singing?

Something **smells** really bad! What is it?

Make up your own questions about the picture. What else is there to see, hear, smell, taste and touch?

Adult help needed!

Touch and guess

What's hiding in the box?

You will need
cardboard box, scissors, different objects

Ask a grown-up to cut a hole in the box and to place different objects inside.

Describe what you feel. Is it rough? Is it smooth? Is it soft, tickly or hard? What is it? Does it bite?!

Ooops, I've turned black and white! Find me in colour on the next page.

Eye trick

Your eyes can play tricks on you.

Look at the blue pattern for a few seconds. Can you see some grey dots?

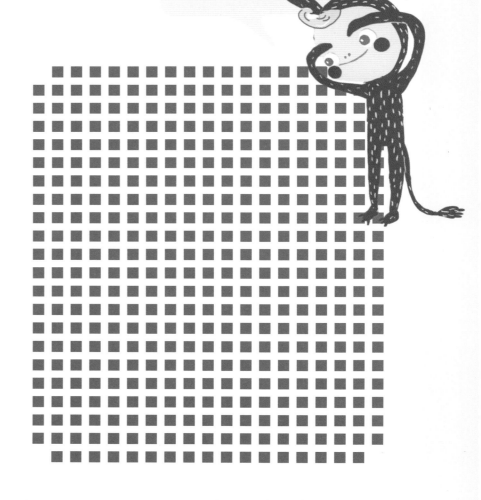

Taste test

What senses do you use when you eat your food?

Adult help needed!

You will need

apple, pear, peeled onion, celery, knife, blindfold

1 Ask a grown-up to chop the food into small pieces.

2 Tie on the blindfold.

3 Pinch your nose. Taste one piece, then another.

This is like when I have a cold. I can't taste anything!

Can you taste the difference? No! Your sense of taste works with your senses of smell and sight to help you enjoy your food.

My hair

What do you think hair is for?

To make us look good?
To help us recognise each other?
To keep us warm? To protect us?
Well, it's all of these things!

Your hair is really strong.

What colour is your hair? Is it fair, brown, red or black?

Some people dye their hair all sorts of colours!

A great way to see how hair grows is when dyed hair grows back. You can see the natural colour at the roots.

An adult's hair grows about 15 cm a year. Look at how long this is on the ruler.

What shape is your hair? Is it straight, wavy or curly?

Older people can lose their hair, or go bald. Can you find a bald person here?

Where next?

Your skin can be different colours, like your hair or eyes.

Go to **My skin, page 40**

Growing up

When you grow up, you grow more hair, especially boys. One day, a boy could grow a moustache or a beard.

Finger moustache

1 Draw a moustache on your finger with a washable felt-tip pen.

2 Try out different designs on each finger.

Moustache postcard

1 Draw a face on a piece of card.

2 Cut out a moustache from furry fabric.

3 Stick the moustache on the face to make your very own moustache character!

25 cm

20 cm

15 cm

10 cm

5 cm

19

My teeth

How do you eat a crunchy snack?

You use your teeth to cut, tear and chew your food into smaller pieces. By the age of six most children have 20 baby teeth. These fall out and 32 adult teeth grow.

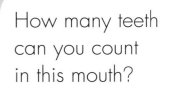

How many teeth can you count in this mouth?

I am falling out!

Front teeth are for cutting. They have sharp edges.

Look! Here's a space for a new tooth.

Oh no! Horrible germs are eating a picnic of leftover food. Germs harm teeth. Better call over the toothbrush.

How tough?

Your teeth are the strongest parts of your body. They're even stronger than your bones!

Hey! I've found a new adult tooth growing here.

It's important to clean your teeth at least twice a day to get rid of all the leftover food.

Don't forget to brush me!

Back teeth are for chewing. They are flatter on top.

21

My voice

Sing your favourite song loudly!

The singing sounds come from inside your throat.
They are made by your vocal cords.

While you are
singing, place your
hand on your throat.
Can you feel your
throat wobbling?

Look! There's a
tube inside with
stretchy parts. These
are your vocal cords.

When you sing,
your vocal cords close
just like in this picture.

When you stop
singing, your vocal
cords open.

 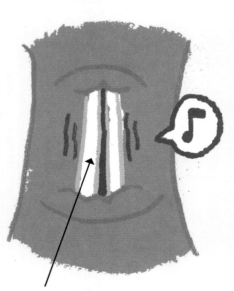 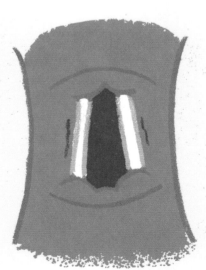

vocal cords closed　　**vocal cords open**

Make voice boxes

High or low?

As you grow, your voice changes. Boys often have lower voices than girls.

You will need

two plastic cups of different widths, four elastic bands

1 Strap two elastic bands across each cup. Put them close together.

2 Pluck them with your fingers to make sounds.

Are the sounds from the two cups different? Which cup makes the lower sound?

Make a paper whistle

You will need

piece of paper 10 cm long and 5 cm wide, scissors

Adult help needed!

Fold the rectangle of paper in half.

Cut out a small triangle on the folded side.

Fold back the two edges and place them against your mouth.

Blow hard!

Where next?

Your body makes lots of sounds.
Go to **Body noises, page 62**

My heart and blood

What beats in your body day and night?

Your heart pumps blood around your body. The blood travels around like a car on a wiggly road.

Where are we?

Let's follow the beating sound.

Trace the journey of the blood with your finger. Follow the arrows.

Blood has many jobs

It warms up your body. = 45

It carries food to every part. = 2

It picks up waste and takes it away. = 2

Look at the picture to find out what else blood does.

What's in blood?

 red blood cells = 25

 white blood cells = 5

 platelets = 9

Find them in the picture. What do they do?

I eat germs.

When your heart beats, it makes a pulse. Press your finger to your wrist to feel your pulse.

Hey! It's a one-way system to the heart.

to the lungs

We're going so fast!

rest of the body

I can feel the heart pushing the blood around!

heart

When you cut yourself, I help to stop the bleeding.

I deliver a useful gas called oxygen.

Beep! Beep! Coming through!

Where next?

Blood picks up good things from the food you eat.

Go to **Eating, page 32**

Cookie people

You will need

plain flour .... 200 g
bicarbonate of soda ...... 1 tsp
butter (cut into bits)....... 100 g
brown sugar................. 75 g
egg 1
golden syrup .... 4 tbsp
mixed spice................. 1 tsp
cinnamon.................... 1 tsp
red and white icing,
dried fruit

Adult help needed!

What to do

1 Preheat the oven to 180°C. Put all the ingredients except the dried fruit and icing into a mixing bowl.

2 Mix into a thick dough with your hands. Roll out the dough to the thickness of your finger.

3 Using a cookie cutter, cut out four people.

4 Place them on a greased baking tray and bake for 10 minutes until golden.

5 Leave to cool. Pipe on red and white icing to show blood travelling through your body.

6 Press on a dried-fruit heart and eat!

Body map

Imagine criss-crossing roads inside your body, delivering blood to every part.

1. Take an old road map and cut out a body shape.

2. Draw on a heart. Can you see how your blood travels now?

Koko's scab story

Koko fell over and cut her knee. She started to bleed, but then her body healed itself!

Oooh! My knee is bleeding. It hurts.

Look! The blood's dried up. I've got a scab.

I'll tell my friends.

blood

a germ

cut

When you scrape your skin, you start to bleed.

HA HA HA

a gang of germs

Then the blood dries and makes a scab.

z z z z

The hard scab stops nasty germs getting into the cut.

Breathing

Ready? Take a deep breath in. Don't forget to breathe out!

Follow the explorers to find out what happens inside your body when you breathe in and out. Start at number 1.

How long can you hold your breath for? Not that long! That's because we must breathe air to stay alive.

Your lungs are like an accordion, sucking in air when you breathe in and pushing it back when you breathe out.

5 You have two lungs, so which way does the air go? It goes both ways!

You breathe in and out all the time, even when you're asleep! Most of the time, you don't even think about it.

6 The insides of your lungs are similar to sponges and take good things from the air.

3 Sometimes the air is dusty. Snot traps the yucky dust and stops it from going any further.

2 Your nose is like a radiator that warms up air.

START

4 Air rushes down to the lungs!

1 When you breathe in, you take air into your mouth and nose. Let's follow the air.

7 Then you breathe out the air that your body doesn't need anymore.

Air from the lungs

There are lots of things we can do with the air that we have in our lungs.

Blow up a balloon. All the air inside has come from your lungs!

When you play a trumpet or horn, you blow air out from your lungs.

Bubble experiment

Air is invisible, but you can see it with this clever trick.

You will need

straw

glass of water

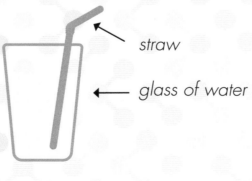

1 Blow through the straw into the glass of water.

2 What can you see? Lots of bubbles filled with air.

Count how long you can blow air bubbles for.

Koko's huff-and-puff experiment

Koko marches up and down the stairs over and over again!
Do you think she starts breathing faster or slower?

When you exercise, you need more air, so your brain
orders you to breathe faster. This gives you the extra air.

Now you try it. But watch out – don't run!

Eating

After you've eaten your dinner, where does all the food go?

Well, it goes on a big adventure through your body! Koko has eaten some vegetables. Take a look inside her body and find out what happens.

Tasty food gives me lots of energy to run around and play!

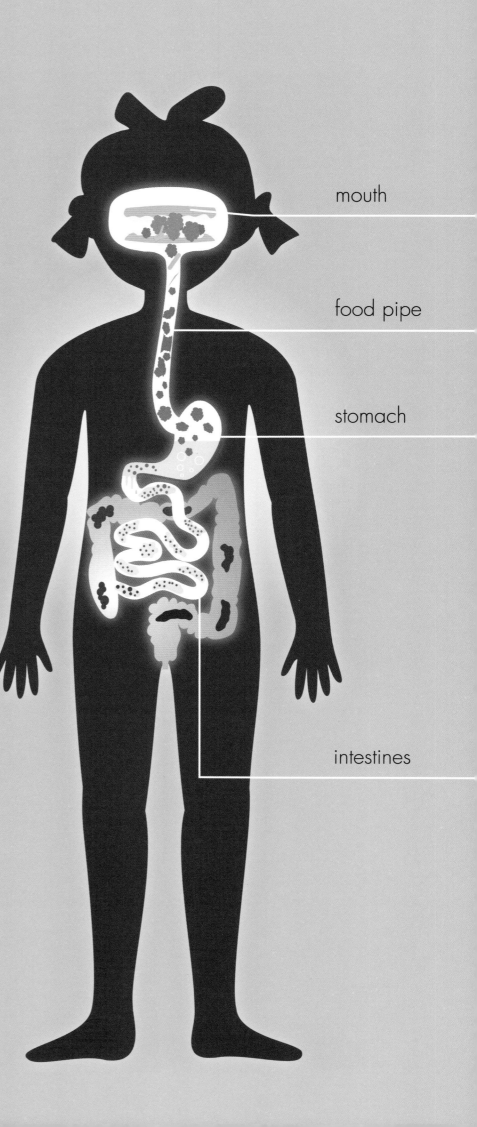

mouth

food pipe

stomach

intestines

Koko cuts and chews the vegetables into small pieces with her teeth. She tastes if the food is salty or sweet with her tongue.

Koko swallows and the pieces go down a long tube.

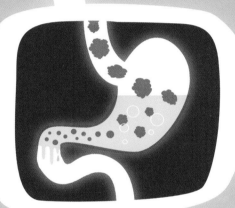

In her stomach, the vegetables mix with juices and break down into even tinier pieces.

These tiny pieces go into a long, wiggly tube called the intestines. Then even tinier bits of food travel in blood around the body.

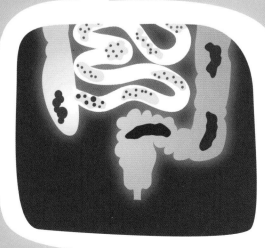

The leftover bits carry on through the tube and come out as poo!

Where next?

Your blood carries the food's good bits around your body.

Go to **My heart and blood, page 24**

33

Spot the foods

Look at what these foods do for you. Find them in the picture.

These foods give you the energy to run and play.

Fruit and vegetables are full of vitamins to keep you healthy.

These foods help your body to grow and mend itself.

Going to the toilet

Play the busy body game!

Food is delivered to different parts of your body. Your body takes the good bits from the food and gets rid of the waste. This waste comes out when you go to the toilet.

You will need

counters

~~a die~~ dice

You can make counters by folding small pieces of paper in half.

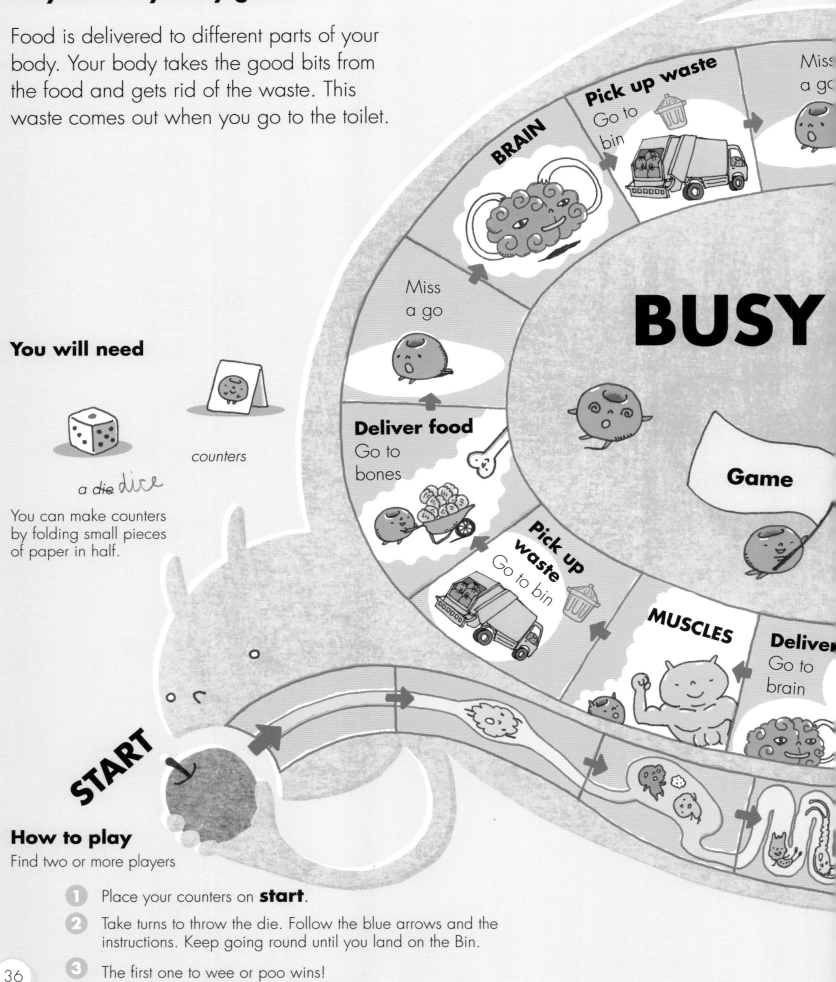

BRAIN

Pick up waste
Go to bin

Miss a go

Miss a go

BUSY

Deliver food
Go to bones

Game

Pick up waste
Go to bin

MUSCLES

Deliver
Go to brain

START

How to play

Find two or more players

1. Place your counters on **start**.

2. Take turns to throw the die. Follow the blue arrows and the instructions. Keep going round until you land on the Bin.

3. The first one to wee or poo wins!

36

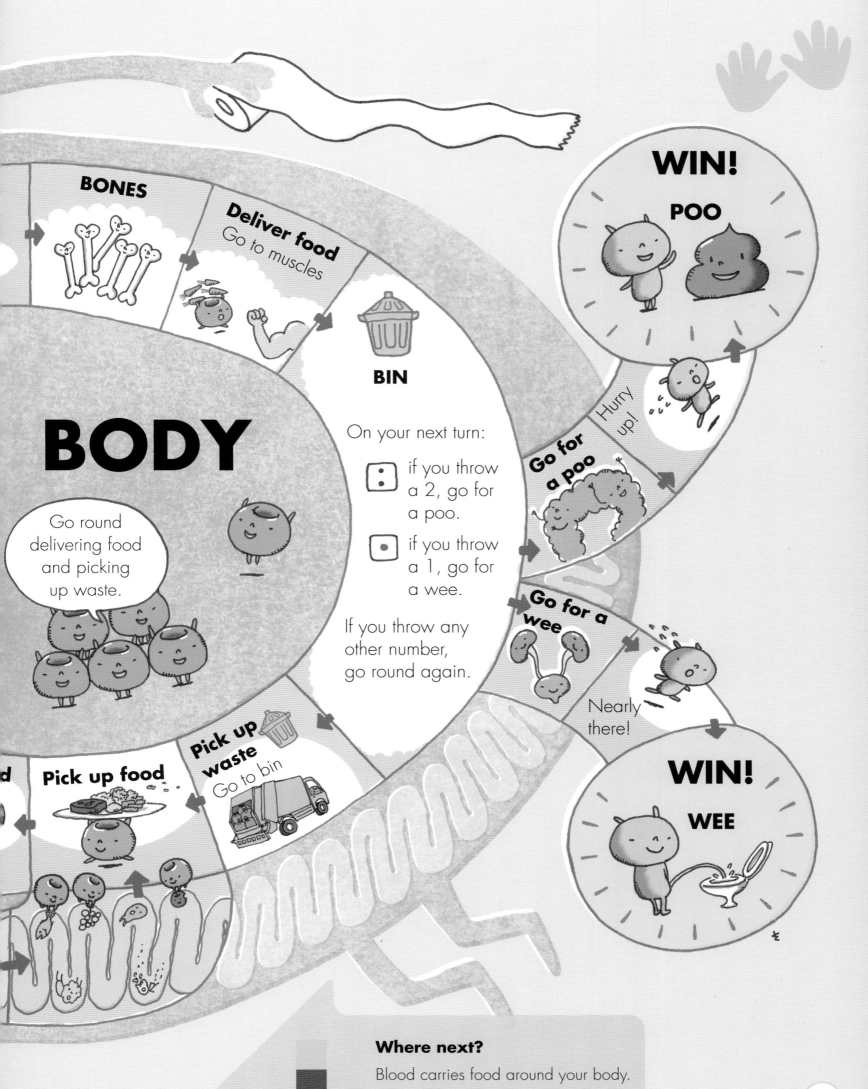

BONES

Deliver food
Go to muscles

BIN

WIN!
POO

BODY

Go round delivering food and picking up waste.

On your next turn:

if you throw a 2, go for a poo.

if you throw a 1, go for a wee.

If you throw any other number, go round again.

Go for a poo

Hurry up!

Go for a wee

Nearly there!

Pick up waste
Go to bin

Pick up food

WIN!
WEE

Where next?

Blood carries food around your body.

Go to **My heart and blood, page 24**

Wee and poo

Did you know that your wee can change colour?

If your wee contains lots of water it is pale yellow.
If it contains lots of waste it is darker yellow.
Most people don't drink water overnight so
their wee is darker first thing in the morning.

We poo throughout our lives ...

Babies poo into
their nappies.

What do you do
while you poo?

Grown-ups poo.
Sometimes they read
while they poo!

Can you match the poo to the owner?
Clue: Koko likes to eat sweetcorn.

Clue: rabbits do tiny poos.

Clue: elephants do giant poos.

Uggh! I've just farted!

He, he! Why does it smell so bad?

Even Grandpa's having a poo.

Everybody farts! Germs eat leftover food in the intestine and make a smelly gas. The gas builds up. It comes out through the bum!

My skin

Your skin covers your whole body and holds it together.

Koko is thinking about her skin and all the ways it looks after her.

My skin is **waterproof**. If it weren't, I'd fill up with water when I have a bath.

My skin is like a suit of armour. It **protects** me from germs.

My skin is **stretchy**. If it weren't, I would be stiff like a scarecrow.

My skin **cools** me down and stops my body from getting too hot in the sun.

My skin lets me **feel**. I can feel the hot sand between my toes.

Fingerprint stamps

Make fingerprint people!

You will need

poster paint or ink pad, paper

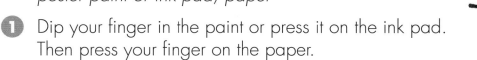

1 Dip your finger in the paint or press it on the ink pad. Then press your finger on the paper.

2 When the prints are dry, draw on arms, legs and faces.

Spot the difference

Everybody has a different fingerprint pattern. Make your print, then ask a friend to do the same. Can you spot the differences?

People have different coloured skin. What colour is yours?

Where next?

Your skin protects you from germs.

Go to **Koko's scab story, page 27**

My bones

Knock knock! The hard parts of your body are your bones.

Together, all your bones make a big frame called a skeleton. Without it, you would be floppy and fall in a heap!

Turn the book around to see a picture of your skeleton.

Here's the skull. It's like a hard helmet protecting your soft brain.

Your ribs protect your heart and lungs.

I found a shoulder bone!

Can you feel the bones in your arm? Point to them on the skeleton.

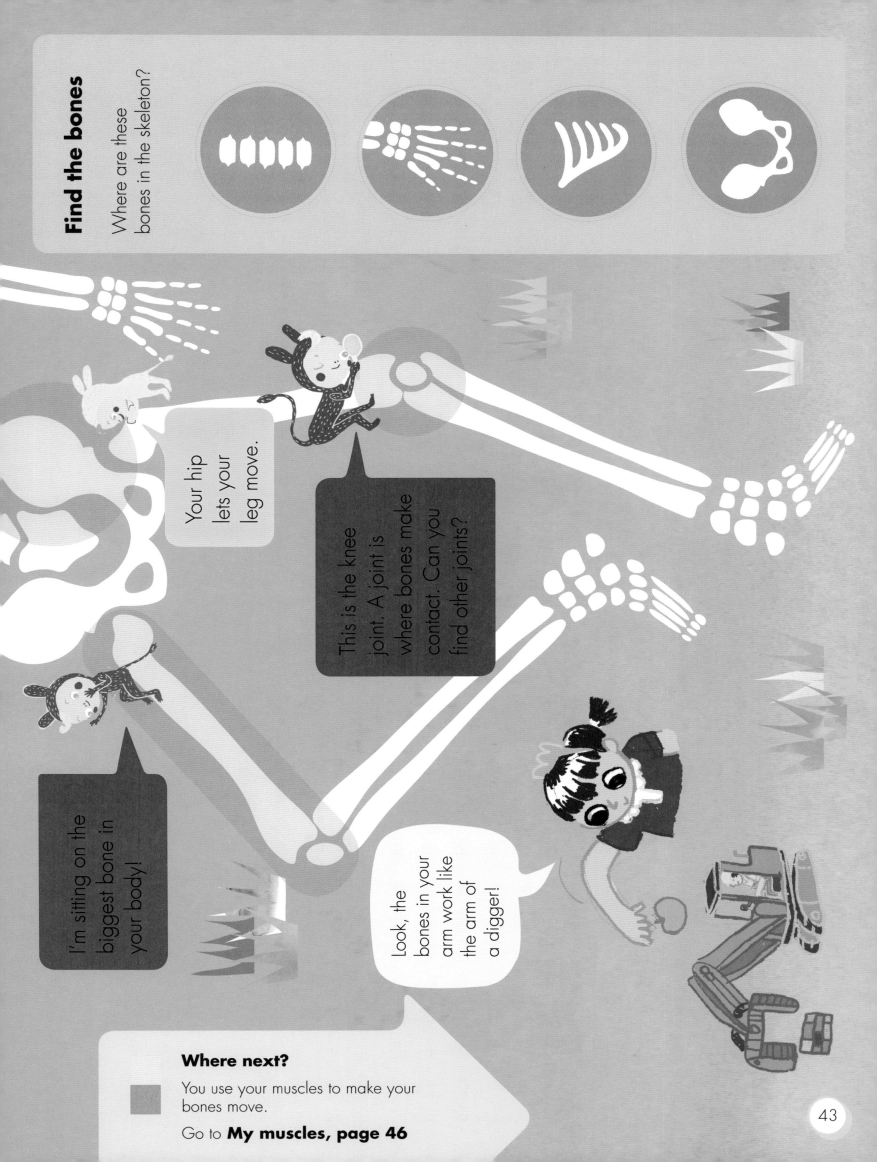

Find the bones

Where are these bones in the skeleton?

Your hip lets your leg move.

This is the knee joint. A joint is where bones make contact. Can you find other joints?

I'm sitting on the biggest bone in your body!

Look, the bones in your arm work like the arm of a digger!

Where next?

You use your muscles to make your bones move.

Go to **My muscles, page 46**

How do I grow?

As you get older, you grow taller.
This is because your bones grow.

1

2

This is Shen …

… and these are her favourite shoes.

3

Wherever Shen went, her shoes went too!

4

Sometimes, Shen and her mum picked up Shen's dad from work. They always walked past Shen's favourite shoe shop.

44

5

One day, Shen could no longer fit into her favourite shoes! They were too tight. What was happening?

6

That night, Shen dreamt her shoes were shrinking. They shrank so much that her teddy bear could wear them!

7

Shen's mum took Shen to her favourite shoe shop. 'The shoes aren't shrinking,' she laughed, 'Your feet are growing! Let's buy a new pair.'

8

Shen loved her new bigger shoes. These were her favourite shoes now. Wherever Shen went, the shoes went too!

My muscles

Can you touch your head and then your toes? Try it now.

Your muscles help to make you move!

Look at all the things we are doing with our muscles!

Ring ring! I'm using my leg muscles to cycle.

Catch! We are using our arm muscles to throw and catch the balls.

We are using lots of muscles when we play at being acrobats.

But how do muscles work?

Muscles pull your bones. They work a bit like the strings on a puppet.

Look at the muscles in my arm! Can you feel your muscles?

Muscle power

This is what happens inside your body when you bend your arm and then straighten it.

bend your arm

Your muscle gets shorter ...

... and the bone gets pulled up.

straighten your arm

Your muscle relaxes ...

... and the bone goes down.

Get moving

Practise each action, then ask a friend to shout out the actions in different orders. If you go wrong, it's your friend's turn!

1 Ready?

2 Do a star jump.

4 Run on the spot.

5 Kick the ball.

6 Swing the racket.

I wonder what is the biggest muscle in your body?

I know. It's your bum and it's called gluteus maximus!

Where next?

Most of your muscles are attached to your bones.

Go to **My bones, page 42**

48

3 Go for a swim.

7 Skate round and round.

Your heart is a muscle too!

How many muscles?

You have about 60 muscles in your face. These muscles help you to pull faces. Pull these faces to show if you are happy, sad, surprised or angry.

What other funny faces can you make?

Body hopscotch game

Let's play a game to make your muscles work!

You will need
a stone
piece of chalk
open space
someone to play with

Get started
Check with an adult first, then draw a body shape on the ground. Split it into squares and number each one.

Adult help needed!

How to play

1 Throw the stone onto square 1 and hop over it to square 2.

2 Hop from numbered square to numbered square up to the head.

3 Turn round and hop back in the same way.

It's your friend's turn if ...

– your stone doesn't land in the right square.
– you hop on the square where your stone is.
– you touch the white lines with your feet.

The winner is ...

the first person to throw the stone onto all eight squares.

4 Pick up the stone and land back at the start. Now try again with the next number!

Try to make your body hopscotch game look like mine!

Staying healthy

Early to rise
for a healthy start,
a healthy body and
a healthy heart!

Healthy food
and lots to drink,
gives your brain
the chance to think.

Take a shower,
run a bath,
splash and swim,
and have a laugh!

Cycle, walk,
skip and run –
healthy sports are
so much fun!

Early to bed
will help you stay,
fit and healthy
every day.

Be kind to others
and watch yourself grow,
happy and healthy from
head down to toe!

Being sick

Everybody feels unwell sometimes.

When you're sick, you go to a doctor in a hospital. What's happening in this hospital? Who's having an eye test? How many bandaged animals can you count? Who has just had babies?

Eye spy

Play eye spy with your friends. To start you off, find …

a fox with its leg in plaster

a duck on the phone

a sick turkey

54

scritch
scratch

RECEPTION

Sleeping

What time do you go to sleep? Do you take a favourite toy to bed with you?

Sleep helps to keep your body healthy and to make you grow.

Try to sleep for 10 or 12 hours each night. You'll feel bright and fresh the next morning!

I'm trying to make the bones grow longer!

Your bones keep growing during the night.

Koko is asleep. What things can you see happening? Do you snore in your sleep like Koko?

Let's finish mashing up this apple and store the energy for tomorrow.

While you are asleep, parts of your body keep working hard.

56

Koko is having a funny dream. Can you remember any of your dreams?

Let's put an elephant in the dream machine!

At night, the brain sorts out all the things you have learnt or seen during the day.

I'm helping to make snoring sounds!

I can see a bruise that needs mending.

Where next?

Your body makes noises when you are asleep and when you are awake.

Go to **Body noises, page 62**

Babies

Where does a baby come from?

A baby comes from its mummy's tummy.

It's hard to imagine, but you were once a tiny baby.

Before you were born, you were so small that you could live inside your mummy!

To make a baby, you need an egg from mummy and a sperm from daddy. The egg and sperm join together to make the baby.

This is what daddy's sperm looks like.

This is what mummy's egg looks like.

sperm   egg

START

When people are grown up, they can have babies!

Look! The tiny baby is starting to grow.

Now the baby is nearly ready to come out of mummy's tummy.

ROUND AND ROUND

Follow the circle round to see the tiny baby grow, be born and become a grown-up.

birth

The baby is born and grows into a toddler.

The toddler grows into a child and then a teenager.

My feelings

How do you feel today? Sing along with this rhyme.

Feeling good, feeling bad, feeling happy, feeling sad.

Feeling stupid, feeling fine, feeling wrong, feeling RIGHT!

Feeling cross, feeling tired, feeling giggly, feeling weird.

Boop!

Feeling little, feeling tall, feeling big, feeling small.

Feeling well, feeling sick, feeling slow, feeling quick.

Feeling sweet, feeling sour, feeling weak, feel my POWER!

Sometimes feeling not a lot, sometimes feeling not sure what.

What a lot of things to feel. Feelings mean we keep it REAL!

61

Body noises

Let's play the noisy game. Burp! We make all kinds of sounds when we are awake and even asleep!

WINNER!

heart beat

nails

NOISY GAME

START

clap

cough

whistle

Make any sound!

click

How to play
A game for two or more players

1. Place your counters on **start**.
2. Take turns to throw the die and move around the board.
3. When you land on a sound, make that noise, then jump to the body part where it comes from (the matching colour on the board).
4. When you land on a body part, go to the sound it makes.
5. When you land on 'Make any sound!', make any body noise you like.
6. The first player to reach the end is the winner!

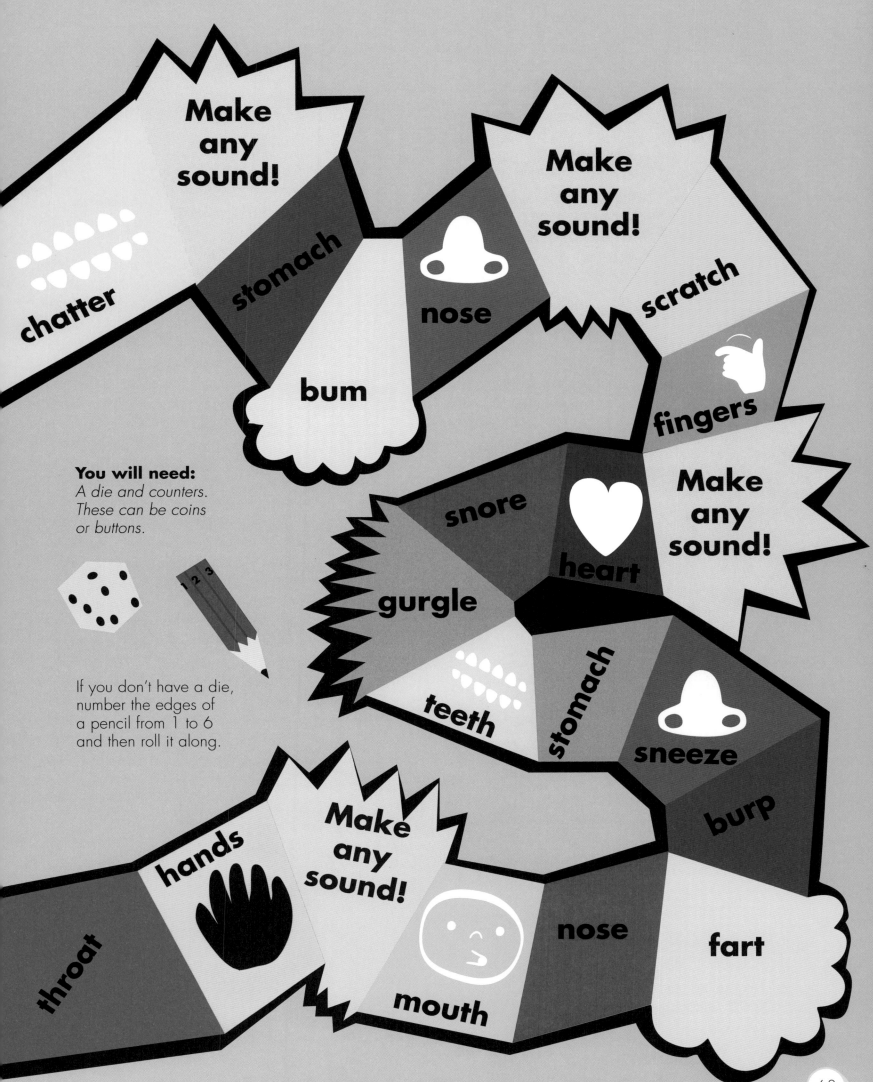

You will need:
A die and counters. These can be coins or buttons.

If you don't have a die, number the edges of a pencil from 1 to 6 and then roll it along.

Index

Look up different parts of the body here and find out the pages they are on. Go through the alphabet to find the word you want.

First published in the United Kingdom in 2012 by Thames & Hudson Ltd, 181A High Holborn, London WC1V 7QX

Copyright © 2012 OKIDO

Photographs Copyright © 2012 Thames & Hudson Ltd, London

All Rights Reserved. No part of this publication may be reproduced or transmitted in any form or by any means, electronic or mechanical, including photocopy, recording or any other information storage and retrieval system, without prior permission in writing from the publisher.

British Library Cataloguing-in-Publication Data
A catalogue record for this book is available from the British Library

ISBN 978-0-500-65000-4

Printed and bound in China by Imago

To find out about all our publications, please visit www.thamesandhudson.com. There you can subscribe to our e-newsletter, browse or download our current catalogue, and buy any titles that are in print.

Produced by OKIDO
the arts and science magazine for kids
www.okido.co.uk

Written by Dr Sophie Dauvois
Illustration by OKIDO Studio: Alex Barrow, Maggie Li and Rachel Ortas
Design OKIDO Studio: Gigi Ho

Additional illustrations:
My brain, My hair, My teeth, Breathing, Going to the toilet, Body hopscotch and Sleeping by Maggie Li
My senses, My heart and blood, How do I grow?, Staying healthy, Babies, My feelings, Body noises, Alex and Koko by Alex Barrow
My muscles and the explorers by Rachel Ortas
Spot the foods and Being sick by Mathilde Nivet
Busy body game by Soju Tanaka
My feelings and Staying healthy poems written by Gabby Dawnay

Special thanks to: Charlotte Brewin, Alice Tabuchi and Miqui Viars for their help; Edmund Fung for the Touch and Guess activity; Emil Gordon and Cleo Ferin for the Moustache postcard; and Emil Gordon and Sabrina Tabuchi for being astronauts.

Science consultant: Dr Jane Maloney, Institute of Education, University of London